IS MARRIAGE in your future?

A 4-week course to h
learn what they nee
c

marriage and family
life later

by Thom and Joani Schultz

Is Marriage in Your Future?
Copyright © 1990 by Group Publishing, Inc.

First Printing

Credits
Edited by Stephen Parolini
Cover designed by Jill Bendykowski and DeWain Stoll
Interior designed by Judy Atwood Bienick and Jan Aufdemberge
Illustrations by Jan Aufdemberge and Judy Atwood Bienick
Cover photo by David Priest and Brenda Rundback
Photo on p. 25 by Jeff Buehler
Photo on p. 46 by Jim Whitmer

ISBN 1-55945-203-X
Printed in the United States of America

CONTENTS

IS MARRIAGE IN YOUR FUTURE?

The family is under siege. Today's teenagers watch from their foxholes as the traditional family of yesteryear falls wounded—the victim of mortar shells launched from every direction. Broken marriages. Shattered promises. Amputated family time. Bombardments of everyday stress.

Each year a million kids in the United States experience their parents' divorce.

But in spite of all the bleak news, teenagers say their top dream in life is to enjoy a good marriage and family life. They've seen the dangers of families under siege, but they cling to the ideal of a man and woman joined in a lifelong commitment of mutual support, dedication and love.

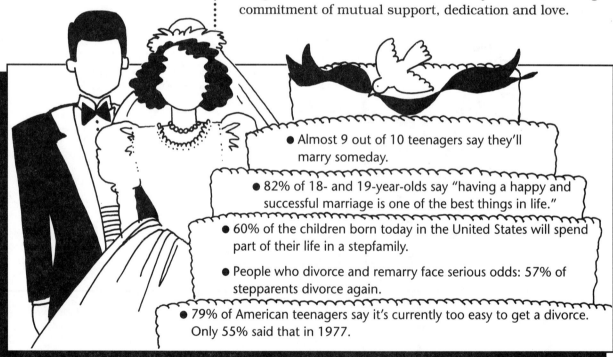

- Almost 9 out of 10 teenagers say they'll marry someday.

- 82% of 18- and 19-year-olds say "having a happy and successful marriage is one of the best things in life."

- 60% of the children born today in the United States will spend part of their life in a stepfamily.

- People who divorce and remarry face serious odds: 57% of stepparents divorce again.

- 79% of American teenagers say it's currently too easy to get a divorce. Only 55% said that in 1977.

Trouble is, teenagers' good intentions and idealism aren't enough to lead them into successful marriages. Before they buy their first car the law requires full disclosure of the terms, conditions and outcome of any loan. With marriage, there's no such full disclosure. Even though the choice to marry someone is one of the biggest decisions they'll face in life, most young people enter into the decision with practically no training or formal guidance. And millions leap into doomed marriages with no preparation and no real inkling of what's required for a lifelong relationship.

This course helps high school kids experience some of the important issues to consider before they say "I do." Now, before they're swept away by tingly feelings of love at first sight, they can think through some crucial ingredients of a successful Christian marriage.

And informed Christian young people who're careful about deciding to marry—and whom to marry—will begin to reverse the dismal family statistics that plague us today.

HOW TO USE THIS COURSE

Think back on an important lesson you've learned in life. Did you learn it from reading about it? from hearing about it? from something you experienced? Chances are, the most important lessons you've learned came from something you experienced. That's what active learning is—learning by doing. And active learning is a key element in Group's Active Bible Curriculum.

Active learning leads students in doing things that help them understand important principles, messages and ideas. It's a discovery process that helps kids internalize what they learn.

Each lesson section in Group's Active Bible Curriculum plays an important part in active learning.

The **Opener** involves kids in the topic in fun and unusual ways.

The **Action and Reflection** includes an experience designed to evoke specific feelings in the students. This section also processes those feelings through "How did you feel?" questions and applies the message to situations kids face.

The **Bible Application** actively connects the topic with the Bible. It helps kids see how the Bible is relevant to the situations they face.

The **Commitment** helps students internalize the Bible's message and commit to make changes in their lives.

The **Closing** funnels the lesson's message into a time of creative reflection and prayer.

When you put all the sections together, you get a lesson that's fun to teach—and kids get messages they'll remember.

● Read the Introduction, the Course Objectives and This Course at a Glance (p. 8).

● Decide how you'll publicize the course using the art on the Publicity Page (p. 9). Prepare fliers, newsletter articles and posters as needed.

● Look at the Bonus Ideas (p. 44) and decide which ones you'll use.

- Read the opening statements, Objectives and Bible Basis for the lesson. The Bible Basis shows how specific passages relate to senior highers today.
- Choose which Opener and Closing options to use. Each is appropriate for a different kind of group. The first option is often more active.
- Gather necessary supplies from This Lesson at a Glance.
- Read each section of the lesson. Adjust where necessary for your class size and meeting room.

BEFORE EACH LESSON

- The approximate minutes listed give you an idea of how long each activity will take. Each lesson is designed to take 35 to 60 minutes. Shorten or lengthen activities as needed to fit your group.
- If you see you're going to have extra time, do an activity or two from the "If You Still Have Time . . . " box or from the Bonus Ideas (p. 44).
- Dive into the activities with the kids. Don't be a spectator. The lesson will be more successful and rewarding to both you and your students.

HELPFUL HINTS

- The answers given after discussion questions are responses your students *might* give. They aren't the only answers or the "right" answers. If needed, use them to spark discussion. Kids won't always say what you wish they'd say. That's why some of the responses given are negative or controversial. If someone responds negatively, don't be shocked. Accept the person, and use the opportunity to explore other angles of the issue.

COURSE OBJECTIVES

By the end of this course your students will:
- explore traits of a good friendship;
- discover how traits in a friendship can keep a marriage together;
- review important questions to ask before marriage;
- define love as a decision, not just a feeling;
- learn that fear is not a good reason to marry; and
- compare a good marriage to God's relationship with us.

THIS COURSE AT A GLANCE

Before you dive into the lessons, familiarize yourself with each lesson aim. Then read the scripture passages.
- Study them as a background to the lessons.
- Use them as a basis for your personal devotions.
- Think about how they relate to teenagers' circumstances today.

LESSON 1: FRIENDS FOREVER

Lesson Aim: To help senior highers discover a good friendship builds the foundation for a good marriage.

Bible Basis: John 15:11-13 and Colossians 3:12-14.

LESSON 2: WHAT MAKES A MARRIAGE WORK?

Lesson Aim: To help students see the importance of compatibility in a marriage.

Bible Basis: 1 Corinthians 11:11-12 and Ephesians 4:2-3.

LESSON 3: WHAT'S LOVE GOT TO DO WITH IT?

Lesson Aim: To help senior highers understand that God's idea of love is more than a feeling—it's a decision.

Bible Basis: 1 Corinthians 13 and 1 John 4:18.

LESSON 4: MARRIAGE IS . . .

Lesson Aim: To help senior highers define marriage as God intended.

Bible Basis: Genesis 2:24 and Ephesians 5:21-33.

PUBLICITY PAGE

G rab your senior highers' attention! Copy this page, then cut and paste the art of your choice in your church bulletin or newsletter to advertise this course on marriage. Or copy and use the ready-made flier as a bulletin insert.

Splash this art on posters, fliers or even post-cards! Just add the vital details: the date and time the course begins, and where you'll meet.

It's that simple.

Is Marriage in Your Future?

A 4-week senior high course on what you need to know now, in order to make good decisions on marriage and family later.

Come to _____

On _____

At _____

Come learn what it takes to prepare for a lifelong, happy marriage.

FRIENDS FOREVER

Making friends is one of the most important skills teenagers strive to develop. But when the thought of marriage pops in kids' heads, they may forget that a lifetime partner can be—and should be—a good friend. Capitalize on this immediate concern for building friendships. Senior highers will be able to relate to that need and apply it to their future.

To help senior highers discover a good friendship builds the foundation for a good marriage.

LESSON AIM

Students will:
- **experience what it's like to work together to complete a task;**
- **explore traits of a good friendship; and**
- **discover how traits in a friendship can keep a marriage together.**

OBJECTIVES

Look up the following scriptures. Then read the background paragraphs to see how the passages relate to your senior highers.

In **John 15:11-13**, Jesus is talking to his disciples about joy.

In this passage, Jesus shares about true joy: loving one another as Christ loves us. He goes on to say that "Greater love has no one than this, that he lay down his life for his friends." And Jesus did just that through the ultimate sacrifice of his life on the cross.

Jesus may not have meant we should all be nailed to a cross or thrown in front of a speeding train to prove our love for our friends. But he may've meant that living a life of love,

BIBLE BASIS
JOHN 15:11-13
COLOSSIANS 3:12-14

service and commitment to our friends shows a deep "Jesus kind of love." What better way to point out to teenagers that the love, service and commitment to a marriage partner can exemplify Jesus' love for us.

In **Colossians 3:12-14**, Paul outlines qualities people of God must "clothe" themselves with.

Because of God's love for us, we in turn show love to others. We do this through compassion, kindness, humility, gentleness, patience, tolerance and forgiveness. All these traits are essential to a good friendship—and a good marriage.

If you ask kids what kind of person they want to marry, they might say someone who's good-looking, rich or funny. These verses help kids look deeper. Teenagers will want to be connected with someone whose friendship qualities let the inner beauty of God's Spirit shine through.

THIS LESSON AT A GLANCE

Section	Minutes	What Students Will Do	Supplies
Opener (Option 1) (Option 2)	up to 5	**What's on the Inside?**—Pick a chocolate and guess what's inside. **Love at First Sight?**—Discuss first impressions people have.	Box of assorted chocolate candies
Action and Reflection	10 to 15	**Lean on Me**—Experience what it's like to work together to complete a task.	
Bible Application	15 to 20	**Friendships and Marriages**—Discuss how the qualities of friendship are important in marriage.	Bibles, pencils, 3×5 cards, newsprint, marker, "What Some Might Say" hand-out (p. 18), tape
Commitment	10 to 15	**I Promise**—Brainstorm practical ways to ensure friendships with potential marriage partners.	Bible
Closing (Option 1) (Option 2)	up to 5	**Thanks, God**—Form a circle and pray for each other. **Circle Celebration**—Join in a celebration of friendship and God's love.	Bible

The Lesson

OPTION 1: WHAT'S ON THE INSIDE?

Pass around a box of assorted chocolate candies. Tell students each to select one candy and hold onto it until everyone gets one. Then have kids each guess what the filling is before they pop it in their mouth. Have students each guess and taste before the next person guesses and tastes. Keep track of how many students guess correctly.

Ask:

● **How did you feel when you guessed correctly or incorrectly?** (Silly; proud; stupid.)

● **How is this experience like finding a friend?** (Sometimes people don't really know a friend that well; some people choose friends by outer appearances only, rather than what that person is like on the inside.)

Say: **Guessing a candy filling can be like choosing someone to be a friend—even a marriage partner. It may seem kind of silly, but in real life a lot of people get married to people they don't know that well. And that could result in a few surprises! A good, solid friendship helps take away those surprises.**

In the next four weeks we'll be studying what to look for in a lifetime partner. You'll learn if you'd make a good marriage partner, and we'll learn some of the secrets to a successful, happy marriage.

OPTION 2: LOVE AT FIRST SIGHT?

If your group is larger than eight, form several groups of no more than eight. Welcome everyone to the class. Ask kids each to think of someone they thought would never be their friend—but now is. Encourage them to tell about first impressions and why those impressions led them to think that person wouldn't be their friend. For instance, Sean might say Pete came off like a real brain and didn't look like he'd be any fun; but once Sean got to know Pete he learned Pete was a great guy to be around. Be open about your own "false impressions."

Ask:

● **What's similar about each person's story?** (Everyone jumped to the wrong conclusion; you can't tell what a person is really like until you get to know him or her.)

● **Is there such a thing as "love at first sight"? Explain.** (No, because you can make mistakes by going on first impressions; no, because people usually grow to love someone.)

● **What do these incidents tell you about finding a marriage partner?** (Don't base your choice on a first impression;

sometimes you're surprised about who becomes your friend or could become your marriage partner.)

Say: **We're launching into a course that asks, "Is marriage in your future?" We often hear that people meet and it's "love at first sight." But as we've just discovered, we can make mistakes by judging someone from first impressions. Let's find out what traits make someone a friend—a friend that could become a lifetime partner.**

ACTION AND REFLECTION
(10 to 15 minutes)

LEAN ON ME

Form pairs. If there's an extra student, become that person's partner and play along.

Have kids introduce themselves and shake hands. Then have them sit back to back on the floor and link elbows. On the count of three, have couples try to stand up. Watch how the couples work together—or fail to! Have students do this exercise a few times to see if they can improve their techniques.

Then ask:

● **How did you feel during this experience?** (Stupid, we couldn't get up; great, we really worked together.)

● **How is this like a friendship?** (We had to work together; we needed to lean on each other for support.)

● **How is this like a marriage?** (Both people need to cooperate to make it work; it's not always easy being connected to another person.)

Comment on what you noticed during the game. For example, did you see some couples give up? Did some carefully plan their strategy before trying to stand? If so, draw parallels to how friendships and marriages operate.

Say: **Mutual support, cooperation and trust are great qualities to have in a friend. And those friendship qualities help build a foundation for a strong marriage. Let's look at a scripture passage that describes lasting friendship qualities and the kind of relationship you'd have with your best friend.**

BIBLE APPLICATION
(15 to 20 minutes)

FRIENDSHIPS AND MARRIAGES

Form groups no larger than five. Ask a volunteer to read aloud Colossians 3:12-14. Encourage kids to follow along in their Bibles.

Hand out pencils and 3×5 cards—enough cards so each person has a card to represent each person in his or her group.

Say: **Colossians says you must "clothe yourselves" with certain qualities. In a moment we're going to "clothe" each other. Each of you has 3×5 cards, one for each person in your group. Please write on one card a friendship quality you see in one of the people in your group. For example, you could write someone is kind or a good lis-**

tener. Continue until you've written a friendship quality for each person on a different card. Refer to Colossians 3:12-14 for ideas. Galatians 5:22-23 has good helps too.

While kids are working, write on separate sheets of newsprint the headings, "Good Friends" and "Marriage Qualities?" Under the heading "Marriage Qualities?" tape the "What Some Might Say" handout (p. 18).

Make sure each group gets tape. Have students decide whose birthday is closest to today. That person will be the first to be clothed with friendship qualities. Have each group member tell what friendship quality describes that person and why, and then tape the card to that person. When finished with one person, have kids continue until each person is clothed in qualities.

After everyone is covered with cards, ask students to bring their qualities forward and tape them under the heading "Good Friends" on the newsprint. Suggest they group similar qualities together. For example, if there are four "good listener" cards, clump them together.

Now read the "Marriages in Trouble" scenarios (p. 16) one by one. After each scenario, look at the two lists of qualities. Ask:

● **Which, if any, of the traits on the "Marriage Qualities?" list would help the couple?** (Probably none of those would help; they're more superficial traits.)

Note: Students might joke, "Yeah, if Patty would've been good-looking, Andy wouldn't have run out on her." Or "If Joel had a lot of money, he and Juanita could make it work." Bring the group around to a serious note by asking if they *really* think good looks or money would help in the long run. If the exercise works as planned, you'll find more helpful characteristics—from Colossians and what the kids wrote under the "Good Friends" heading. Ask:

● **Which, if any, of the items on the "Good Friends" list would help the couple?** (Loyal; trustworthy; is a good listener; helps with problems.)

As students find "Good Friends" qualities that would help a couple, have someone tear the drawing of the couple from the "What Some Might Say" handout and tape it near those words.

After all the scenarios have been read, ask:

● **What did you discover about what makes a good marriage?** (Qualities of a friend; characteristics God says you should clothe yourself with.)

● **Why is friendship so vital to a marriage?** (You can trust a friend; friends stick by you no matter what.)

● **What do you have to invest in a friendship to make it work?** (Time; risks.)

● **How is that like what two people invest in a marriage?** (They need to spend time together; they need to communicate often.)

Good Friends

Marriage Qualities (what some might say)

1. *Good Personality*
2. *Sense of Humor*
3. *Good looks*
4. *Intelligence*
5. *artistic ability + Sensitivity*
6. *Money*

Wrap up the discussion by asking a volunteer to read aloud Colossians 3:12-14.

Marriages in Trouble

Help! These couples are in trouble. What qualities do they need to mend their breaking relationships?

Couple #1—Andy finally admitted to Patty that he'd been cheating on her. All those times he said he was working late, he was really seeing another woman. What does this couple need?

Couple #2—Juanita and Joel never talk. It's just easier that way. It seems whenever the two of them start discussing something they end up fighting. What does this couple need?

Couple #3—Bev works a lot. She admits she's a workaholic. That means she always chooses work over time with Harvey. Harvey resents all the time Bev spends at her job. It's like they hardly know each other anymore. What does this couple need?

Couple #4—Wendy loves to talk. She's always got something she can't wait to tell Keith. But Keith comes home so bushed from working all day, he can't wait to relax and tune out the world. Wendy wants to talk, but Keith always wants it to wait. "I'm too tired, honey" or "Can't that wait until tomorrow?" are his favorite lines. Wendy's frustrated because tomorrows never come. What does this couple need?

COMMITMENT
(10 to 15 minutes)

I PROMISE

Say: **Before we start thinking marriage—imagining the white picket fence, two kids, a station wagon, a dog and wedded bliss—we need to remember the importance of a couple being best friends. Imagine if this dream person were of the same sex, would you be that person's best friend?**

Jesus described the greatest love as laying down your life for a friend. Marriage is the ultimate in giving your life to someone.

Have someone read aloud John 15:13.

Ask students each to get back together with their original partner from Lean on Me. Have partners sit knee to knee facing each other. Say: **Imagine you've just met someone you think you'd like to marry. Tell your partner how you intend to build a strong and lasting friendship with that person. What specifically can you do to make sure the two of you will be best friends. For example, you may decide not to rush into anything and give your relationship a chance to mature over time. Or you might plan to have that person join in your family activities each Sunday afternoon.**

Allow time for pairs to share. If time permits, have students report to the whole group practical ideas they came up with.

OPTION 1: THANKS, GOD

Have class members stand in a circle holding hands. Ask them to scan the "Good Friends" list from Friendships and Marriages. Have students each look for a friendship quality that best describes the person on their right. Go around the circle and have each person add a prayer of thanks for the person on their right:

"Thank you, God for _____. He/she is a good friend because _____." For example, "Thank you, God for Elise. She's a good friend because she's so loyal."

Conclude by reading aloud John 15:13, and thanking Jesus for giving his life for us—his friends.

OPTION 2: CIRCLE CELEBRATION

Form a circle with students standing with their arms at their sides.

Pray: **God, we thank you for the gift of friendship. To acknowledge that gift we join hands.** (Join hands.) **Thanks for the joy a marriage can bring when a man and a woman decide to share a lifetime of friendship. To show that joy, let's put our arms around each other.** (Put arms around each other.) **Thanks for being our friend forever through marriage or singleness. We celebrate that you've given your life for us. For you've said, "Greater love has no one than this, that he lay down his life for his friends."**

We praise you for that eternal love and friendship. To celebrate that love, let's hug one another until I say, "Amen." (Hug each other, and when appropriate, shout, "Amen!")

If You Still Have Time ...

Marriages They Know—Have students tell about someone they know whose marriage is based on friendship. Talk about what's good about that. Without giving names, have them compare those marriages with marriages they know that aren't based on friendship.

God's Idea—Give each student a piece of string or yarn. Have kids each form it into a shape that describes God's idea of a perfect marriage. Have them explain their formations.

What Some Might Say

A national magazine asked teenagers which of these qualities were important to them in a relationship with the opposite sex. They listed these:

Good Personality

Sense of Humor

Good Looks

Intelligence

Artistic ability/Sensitivity

Money

Patty and Andy

Bev and Harvey

Juanita and Joel

Wendy and Keith

WHAT MAKES A MARRIAGE WORK?

Many young people today spend more time researching and investigating the college they want to attend than researching and investigating the person they end up marrying. What a shame!

We can give young people a lifelong gift by teaching them to discern compatibility in a possible mate.

To help students see the importance of compatibility in a marriage.

LESSON AIM

Students will:
● **plan a wedding with someone who probably differs in values and background;**
● **review important questions to ask before marriage; and**
● **create a marriage vow from scripture.**

OBJECTIVES

Look up the following scriptures. Then read the background paragraphs to see how the passages relate to your senior highers.

In **1 Corinthians 11:11-12**, Paul writes about the interdependence a man and woman have with each other.

Men and women need each other. These verses explain the cyclical nature that woman was made from man and man is born of woman. The verse culminates with: "But everything comes from God."

Teenagers can see that one sex isn't meant "to lord over the

BIBLE BASIS
1 CORINTHIANS 11:11-12
EPHESIANS 4:2-3

other." According to God's plan we're interdependent creatures who need to accept each other and learn to live together in harmony. And that's a "marriage" message to be sure.

In **Ephesians 4:2-3**, Paul urges his readers to be humble, gentle, patient and tolerant.

In these verses, Paul emphasizes the importance of humility, gentleness, patience and tolerance for preserving the unity of the spirit in the church.

Marriage is a super example of the "unity of the Spirit." When two people join as one, they pool a lot of differences that need tolerating. You can point senior highers toward the truth that two people usually bring two very different worlds together. These worlds consist of faith, values, family backgrounds and traditions. The best marriages are those that celebrate—and tolerate—the differences.

THIS LESSON AT A GLANCE

Section	Minutes	What Students Will Do	Supplies
Opener (Option 1)	5 to 10	**Give Me One Good Reason**—Tell why they'd make good marriage partners.	3×5 cards, pencils
(Option 2)		**Crazy Caveman Club**—Pretend to be "Cavepeople" selecting mates.	Newspaper
Action and Reflection	15 to 20	**Plan Your Wedding Day**—Experience planning a wedding and discuss compatibility.	Paper, scissors, pencils, newsprint, marker, "Before You Ask, 'Will You Marry Me?' " handouts (p. 25)
Bible Application	10 to 15	**Create-a-Vow**—Read scriptures and write a wedding vow.	"Verses for Vows" handouts (p. 26), pencils, Bibles
Commitment	5 to 10	**Compatibility**—Read and complete a certificate of commitment.	"Certificate of Commitment" handouts (p. 26), pencils
Closing (Option 1)	up to 5	**A Good Mix**—Compare a variety of liquids with good and bad marriages.	Glass pitcher of water, a glass, cooking oil, pre-sweetened lemonade mix, long spoon, cups
(Option 2)		**My Partner**—Tell why their partner would make a good spouse for someone.	

The Lesson

OPENER
(5 to 10 minutes)

OPTION 1: GIVE ME ONE GOOD REASON

Pass out two 3×5 cards and a pencil to each person. Tell students each to write on a card one reason they'd make a good marriage partner. For example, "I'm a good listener" or "I do dishes without complaining." After they've written their reasons, have them each sign their card. Collect the cards and number them.

Have kids list numbers down one side of their extra card to match the number of students in the classroom. Next, begin with the #1 card and read one reason at a time. Have kids guess who wrote each reason. After you've read all the reasons, go back and have kids tell their answers. Reveal each person's identity and reason one by one. Enjoy a few laughs as you learn more about each other.

Say: **We've just found out some interesting facts about each other. Especially facts that make us think somebody would be pretty lucky to have us as a mate! This lesson will focus on what makes a marriage work.**

OPTION 2: CRAZY CAVEMAN CLUB

Say: **There's a legend that says cavemen clubbed their wives as a sign of their affection. Well, here's your chance!**

Have kids sit in a circle of chairs. Choose one person to be the "clubber." Roll up a newspaper lengthwise so it makes a flimsy club. Have the person who's the clubber wander around the circle and choose a cave mate by gently "clubbing" that person over the head and dropping the club.

Have the "clubbee" chase the clubber around the circle. The clubber runs around the circle to the empty chair of the clubbee before the clubbee retaliates with a whack of the paper club. If the clubber isn't clubbed on the way around, the clubbee then becomes the clubber. If the clubber gets clubbed, he or she must try again—maybe with another cave mate this time! Encourage everybody to add prehistoric grunts and cheers.

Enjoy a few wacky rounds of the game. Say: **The art of choosing a mate has come a long way. Today few mates prefer to be chosen by being clubbed over the head! We're going to take a look at what makes a marriage work in this day and age. Say goodbye to clubs and hello to compatibility.**

ACTION AND REFLECTION

(15 to 20 minutes)

PLAN YOUR WEDDING DAY

Make enough slips of paper to equal the number of students in the class. Number pairs of slips with matching numbers. For instance, two cards will be numbered 1, two others will be numbered 2, and so on. Make a code mark per pair to designate who'll be the bride in the couple. For example, label the first pair 1 and 1B.

Tell the class that a sophisticated computer-dating service will select who in this class would make great couples. Randomly distribute the slips of paper. Then tell students about the code. Say: **You must find the person who matches your number. Once you've gotten your match, see who has the "B." That person gets to be the lucky bride!**

Be prepared for bursts of laughter, since the matching may or may not have paired them male and female. Say something about modern technology's quirks.

Give couples paper and pencils. Then say: **We're about to find out about some of your quirks, values and dreams. For the next five minutes, you'll plan as much of your wedding as time allows. Don't pretend to be somebody else. Be yourself and give your actual opinions. For example, maybe you've thought about having a big wedding or a small wedding or even eloping. The two of you must decide together what plans you'll make as if the two of you were combining your wishes to plan a real wedding.**

Write the following questions on newsprint, and tell pairs to include the answers to these questions in their plans.

1. How long will your engagement be?
2. When will your wedding be held?
3. Where will your wedding be held?
4. How big will your wedding be?
5. What colors and flowers will you select?
6. Where will your honeymoon be?

Say: **Write your final plans on your paper. Remember, you're a couple and you must come to a consensus. Go!**

Pressure students to finish quickly. That will enhance the feeling of frustration. When couples are finished, ask for a few wedding plans. Thank them for their hard work; then form groups no larger than six.

Ask:

● **How did you feel during this exercise?** (Frustrated.)

● **How was this activity similar to planning a real wedding?** (It's not easy to compromise; there's too much to do.)

● **What were examples of when you agreed, disagreed or compromised?** (We both wanted a big wedding; one of us wanted a big wedding and the other wanted to elope.)

● **What did this exercise tell you about two people's backgrounds coming together for a marriage?** (One person may have to give in; people each have their own ideas about how things should be done.)

Have students each tell what they appreciated about how their partner handled compromising and working together.

2. ✗

Say: **Have you ever heard the phrase "opposites attract"? There may be some truth in that, but most lifelong marriages are built on what partners have in common, not what they disagree about. Sure, it's fine to have some differences such as one partner likes winter, the other likes fall. But there can be real trouble if one is a devoted Christian and the other a devoted atheist. A starting point for a good marriage is selecting the right person. Let's explore important questions two people must discuss before making marriage plans.**

Give students the "Before You Ask, 'Will You Marry Me?' " handout (p. 25). Have original couples pair up again and iron out as many questions from one category as they can. If time allows, have couples discuss another category. For variety, assign different couples different categories.

CREATE-A-VOW

Ask students:

● **How'd you feel about discussing those questions with your partner?** (It felt weird; I felt closer to my partner.)

● **Why do you suppose so many couples never discuss these questions before they marry?** (It could be touchy; couples don't want to deal with areas they don't agree on.)

● **How important for a lasting marriage is a couple's agreement to these questions?** (Very important; pretty important, people can disagree and still be married.)

Say: **There's a lot to think about before taking the plunge into a lifelong commitment. Save your handout for future use. It can become an invaluable tool if marriage is in your future.**

Now it's time to search God's Word for what's important in marriage. I'll give you a list of Bible verses. Look up those verses and create a wedding vow with your partner. The vow can be a sentence or several sentences. The vow becomes a promise two people make to each other when they commit to marrying each other.

Give people each a "Verses for Vows" handout (p. 26), a pencil and a Bible. Have pairs complete their handouts and read their vows to the group.

Ask:

● **What did you learn about marriage by writing a vow?** (The Bible can provide a good basis for a wedding promise.)

● **What's God's idea of a perfect marriage?** (Two people becoming one; two people serving each other.)

COMPATIBILITY

Have partners sit facing each other. Pass out the "Certificate of Commitment" (p. 26) and a pencil to each person. Allow time for partners to discuss and fill in the certificate.

Have partners read aloud their commitment to each other.

BIBLE APPLICATION
(10 to 15 minutes)

COMMITMENT
(5 to 10 minutes)

Table Talk

The Table Talk activity in this course helps senior highers discuss with their parents what makes a good marriage.

If you choose to use the Table Talk activity, this is a good time to show students the "Table Talk" handout (p. 27). Ask them to spend time with their parents completing it.

Before kids leave, give them each the "Table Talk" handout to take home, or tell them you'll be sending it to their parents.

Or use the Table Talk idea found in the Bonus Ideas (p. 45) for a meeting based on the handout.

CLOSING
(up to 5 minutes)

OPTION 1: A GOOD MIX

Place a glass pitcher of water on a table. Pour a bit of water into a glass. Then pour into the glass some cooking oil and stir. Have students compare the oil and water to people who aren't compatible in marriage.

Next bring out presweetened lemonade mix. Pour that into the pitcher and stir. Compare the mixing to a good marriage. Pour a cup of lemonade for each person. Before the class members drink, conclude with a prayer of thanksgiving for the gift of good marriages. Pray also that students make wise choices in their future. Have teenagers hold up the cups, and close with a toast to successful marriages.

OPTION 2: MY PARTNER

Have senior highers form pairs. If there's an extra person, pair up with the student yourself. Stand in a circle and have kids each tell why their partner would make a good spouse for someone. Have students close with a one- or two-sentence prayer highlighting the lesson's discoveries.

If You Still Have Time . . .

The Great Debate—Challenge kids to decide if there's only one person in the whole world who's meant for them.

Both Ends of the Aisle—Draw an imaginary aisle down the center of the classroom. Read aloud the following statements and designate one end of the aisle to mean "I agree" and the other, "I disagree." Students can stand anywhere along the aisle that best represents their opinion.

1. A Christian and a non-Christian can have a good marriage.

2. Spouses should get permission from each other to spend more than $10 on a purchase.

3. Couples who know each other sexually before marriage have a better chance of a successful marriage.

4. Spouses should tell each other everything.

BEFORE YOU ASK,
"Will You Marry Me?"

Family Questions
- Do you both want children? If so, how many?
- Would both of you feel good about adopting children if you couldn't have children of your own?
- What's your philosophy about raising children? How would you discipline them? reward them?
- Who will do the cooking? cleaning? laundry? shopping? yardwork? carrying out the garbage? vehicle maintenance?
- How much time should each of you spend with friends?

Faith Questions
- Are you both Christians? How will that affect your marriage?
- How do your families view the Christian faith? the church?
- Do you both come from similar church backgrounds? How may that affect your marriage?
- Will you worship together? How often?
- Will you do family devotions? meal prayers? Bible reading?

Money Questions
- Do you plan to work out a detailed monthly spending budget before you're married?
- What proportion of your monthly income will you put in savings?
- How much money will you give to the church? to charities?
- Should you get permission from each other before you spend any money?
- How do you feel about borrowing money from your parents or other relatives?

Sex Questions
- How do you feel about birth control?
- Do you feel comfortable with who initiates physical affection in your relationship?
- How often do you think a married couple should have sexual intercourse?
- If you had sexual problems would you seek professional help?
- If sexual intercourse became impossible (for example, through paralysis or impotency), could your marriage continue effectively?

Communication Questions
- Do you always believe everything your partner tells you?
- What topics are off-limits because they cause conflict? Is it possible to endure an entire lifetime without dealing with those topics?
- When you have a conflict with your partner, do you typically talk about it, shout it out, clam up or use physical force? How would your two styles of handling conflict mix in a marriage?
- How much should you know about what your partner does when he or she is away from you?

Save this list of questions. Use them to get better acquainted with a friend that could become a lifetime partner.

VERSES FOR VOWS

Read these verses about how God is central to the marriage commitment before you create a wedding vow.

- Genesis 1:27-28
- Genesis 2:23-24
- Matthew 6:19-21
- 1 Corinthians 10:24
- 1 Corinthians 11:11-12
- 2 Corinthians 4:16-18
- Ephesians 4:2-3
- Ephesians 5:21-33

Our Wedding Vow

CERTIFICATE OF COMMITMENT

I,_____, being of sound mind and body, do hereby promise that if I ever decide to get married, I will not rush into a marriage until I've carefully and thoroughly determined a high degree of compatibility with my potential mate. I will thoroughly and completely discuss with my future mate the issues of family, faith, money, sex and communication.

Signed:_____   Date:_____

Witness:_____   Date:_____

Table Talk

To the Parent: We're involved in a senior high course at church called, "Is Marriage in Your Future?" Students are learning what makes a good marriage that pleases God. We'd like you and your teenager to spend some time discussing this important topic. Use this sheet to help you do that.

Parent
- The best thing about marriage is . . .
- The worst thing about marriage is . . .
- What I wish I would've known about marriage when I was a teenager . . .
- I think God smiles on marriage because . . .

Teenager
- The perfect mate is someone who . . .
- I think I will/won't marry in the future because . . .
- I need to marry someone who . . .
- Marriage is/isn't scary to me because . . .

Parent and teenager

Tell if you agree or disagree with each statement below. Then give reasons for your answer.
- Marriage is for a lifetime.
- It's more important to love a spouse than to like him or her.
- A husband and wife should be each other's best friend.
- Christian marriages don't have problems.
- A husband and wife should be seen as complete equals in a marriage relationship.

Here are five important marriage issues. Rank them from 1 through 5 (1=the most important). Compare your answers with each other and explain your rankings.

Parent(s)		Teenager
____	Sex	____
____	Money	____
____	Faith	____
____	Communication	____
____	Commitment	____

Together read aloud Ephesians 5:21-33. Then discuss these questions:
- Why does God compare marriage to a relationship with Christ?
- What does it mean to submit yourselves to one another because of your reverence to God?
- What's the difference between love and respect?
- What does "the two will become one" mean?

LESSON 3

WHAT'S LOVE GOT TO DO WITH IT?

In a media-saturated society, images of love and marriage barrage kids every day. But not all those images are good. Most of them say love is a feeling. And that feeling—or lack of it—can completely drive your decisions and actions. It's true that love is a feeling, but when it comes to marriage, love is much more than that. Love is a decision, a commitment, a promise to last a lifetime.

LESSON AIM

To help senior highers understand that God's idea of love is more than a feeling—it's a decision.

OBJECTIVES

Students will:
- see love as a decision, not just a feeling;
- learn that fear is not a good reason to marry; and
- discover God's idea of genuine love.

BIBLE BASIS
1 CORINTHIANS 13
1 JOHN 4:18

Look up the following scriptures. Then read the background paragraphs to see how the passages relate to your senior highers.

In **1 Corinthians 13**, Paul unfolds a definition of love. The Apostle Paul wrote this letter to the church at Corinth. He wanted to help them work through concerns about divisions in the church. Through this love passage, Paul presents God's perfect love as one of God's best gifts to human beings.

Teenagers "fall" in love. They fall out of love. Adolescent "love" can be confusing. This chapter helps put love in perspective. It gives kids an ideal to strive for in a relationship.

In **1 John 4:18**, the author writes how love drives out fear.

In the preceding verses to this passage, God is defined with one word: "love." The verses follow with our motive for love: "We love because he first loved us." Verse 18 explains "perfect love" by saying there's no fear in perfect love. Although this love passage isn't specifically speaking of marriage, it holds up the greatest example of love two people can model.

Since perfect love doesn't involve fear, we can help teenagers see that if it's time to make a lifetime commitment in marriage, they must make it out of love—not fear. This isn't to say there's not a fear of the unknown when people decide to marry. It does say fear shouldn't be the motive for marriage.

THIS LESSON AT A GLANCE

Section	Minutes	What Students Will Do	Supplies
Opener (Option 1)	5 to 10	**Blinded Bride**—Play a game and experience what it's like to blindly search for a marriage partner.	Blindfold
(Option 2)		**Honey, If You Love Me**—Play a game and discuss what it's like to be pressured to do something.	
Action and Reflection	10 to 15	**Fact or Feeling?**—Experience what it's like to rely on feelings instead of facts.	"Love Is More Than a Feeling" handouts (p. 34)
Bible Application	15 to 20	**Perfect Love Casts Out Fear**—Role-play marriage counseling experiences.	Bibles, "Perfect Love—or Not?" handouts (p. 35), scissors
Commitment	5 to 10	**True Love**—List good reasons a couple might decide to love one another enough to get married.	Newsprint, marker, Bible, tape
Closing (Option 1)	up to 5	**God's Love for Me**—Pray for one another using a prayer based on 1 John 4:9-11.	
(Option 2)		**The Love Prayer**—Pray as scripture is read.	Bible

The Lesson

OPTION 1: BLINDED BRIDE

Have students stand at various points in the room. Blindfold one person to be the "bride" in search of a "groom." Spin the person around. Tell the bride to call out, "Will you marry me?" Silently select one person to be the groom. It's that per-

OPENER
(5 to 10 minutes)

son's job to disguise his or her voice and answer the bride's call with "I will." Everyone in the group, including the groom, tries *not* to be touched by the bride during his or her search. The other students can move around the room but they can't speak. The bride must call out and try to touch the designated groom. If the bride does find the groom, blindfold another person to search.

Observe the group's reaction during the game. When finished, gather together and ask:

● **How did you feel during the game as the bride? the groom? the rest of the group?** (Silly; frustrated; wanting to help the bride.)

● **How was our experience like or unlike people searching for a mate?** (It's similar because some people grab the first person that comes along; it's different because people searching for a mate can see who they're going after.)

Say: **We're going to look at why people decide to marry. Marriage is a huge, lifelong commitment to another person. That decision deserves a lot of time, thought and prayer. Next we're going to do something to show you what that decision means.**

OPTION 2: HONEY, IF YOU LOVE ME

Ask students to sit in a circle. Have a volunteer sit on someone's lap and ask, "Honey, if you love me won't you please, please smile?" Without cracking a smile, the person must respond, "I love you honey, but I just can't smile." If the person does break down and smile, that person becomes the next asker. If the person maintains a straight face, the asker must go to another person and get a smile. Play a few rounds and have fun.

When finished, ask:

● **How did you feel about someone asking you to do something you didn't want—or weren't supposed—to do?** (Pressured; glad I was asked.)

● **We asked, "Honey, if you love me won't you please, please smile?" What other kinds of things do people ask of each other to prove their love?** (If you love me you'll have sex; you'll lie to your parents about what really happened.)

Say: **We love to be loved. And we love to have people prove their love to us. It's important that we understand what love is all about. Next we're going to do something that'll help us better understand love.**

Note to the teacher: To be successful with the next experience, practice it with another person before class. You'll want to do it, so you'll actually believe it works. It's weird!

FACT OR FEELING?

Ask for one volunteer to sit on a chair in front of the class. Stand beside the chair and have the volunteer sit with eyes closed. Ask the rest of the class to remain silent while you proceed. Hold your hand about a foot above the volunteer's head. Snap your fingers and ask the volunteer to tell you after each snap where the sound is coming from—the front or back. If you can't snap your fingers, clap or strike a spoon against a glass.

Keep your hand equidistant between the listener's ears, alternating your snaps from front to back. Or do a few in the same position to trick the person into thinking you might've moved. Ask the person each time where the sound is coming from. (Normally people are unable to accurately tell where the sound is coming from.)

After the experiment, have the volunteer open his or her eyes. Reveal to the person—with the class's help—where the snaps were coming from. The volunteer probably won't believe you! The experience is deceiving and is fun to watch too.

Depending on the class size, you may want to have other volunteers try it. Or have students pair up and do the experiment themselves.

Ask:

● **How did you feel during the experiment?** (Amused; surprised.)

● **How did you feel when you were told you were wrong?** (I couldn't believe it; I felt deceived and tricked.)

● **What does this teach you about trusting your feelings?** (It's easy to be tricked by feelings.)

Say: **Sometimes we can be absolutely convinced by how we feel. Our first volunteer was certain the sound was coming from the front when it was coming from behind.** (Or vice versa.) **Those decisions were based on feelings. Our volunteer went into the decision with eyes closed.**

Many people, when asked why they decided to get married, say, "It felt right" or "We felt so much in love."

Ask:

● **How was our experience like people who say "It felt right" or "We felt so much in love"?** (Sometimes you're right, sometimes you're wrong.)

Give senior highers the responsive reading, "Love Is More Than a Feeling" (p. 34). Read it together. After the reading, pair up students guy/girl, guy/girl as much as possible. Encourage pairs each to select two statements from the reading they most agree or disagree with and tell why.

Have partners report back what they learned.

PERFECT LOVE CASTS OUT FEAR

Ask someone to read aloud 1 John 4:18.

Say: **Basing love on a decision instead of feelings isn't easy. That's because the warm feelings of being in love**

are great. Those feelings are a gift from God. We need to make sure they're not the only grounds for marriage.

Sometimes fear keeps people from making clear-headed choices about love and marriage. How can couples know their marriage doesn't hinge on fear? We're going to find out by searching scripture.

Cut apart the "Perfect Love—or Not?" handout (p. 35). Form pairs. Say: **I have four case studies from couples who're deciding whether to get married. These couples have come to premarital counseling to get advice. They want to know they're getting married for the right reasons. All the couples believe they should go ahead with their marriage plans. But the counseling will help them see all sides of the issue.**

I'll give each couple one of the case studies. Half of the pairs will be couples and the other half will be counselors. I'll match up two counselors per couple. Here's your task: Couples, read the scripture verses and develop arguments that convince the counselors you're getting married for the right reasons—not out of fear. Counselors, read the verses and advise the couple not to get married because you're not sure they've thought through everything.

Hand out the case studies, making sure couples each have a counselor pair assigned to their case. If your group is small, kids don't need to work in pairs. If your group is large, have some couples and counselors working on the same case studies. Allow couples and counselors a couple of minutes to read over their case studies and look up the scriptures.

Place four chairs at the front of the classroom to set the stage for the counseling session. After everyone's ready, say: **Imagine we're at Holy Matrimony Counseling Services. It's a unique set-up because we can watch the counseling sessions through this one-way glass.**

Point out an imaginary window that divides the front of the class from the class members.

Say: **We can see the people, but they can't see us. Each couple will come up here and talk with the counselors. Let's get started.**

Invite a couple and counseling pair for each case study. Remind the class members that they're "listening in." Have the couple present its views and have the counselors respond. Call time after a minute or two. At the end of the "counseling session," have the couples tell whether they still plan to marry. Remind kids that love is a decision strengthened by careful thinking, prayer and a commitment as God intended.

Table Talk Follow-Up

If you sent the "Table Talk" handout (p. 27) to parents last week, discuss students' reactions to the activity. Ask volunteers to share what they learned from the discussion with their parents.

TRUE LOVE

Form groups of four or less. Give each group a sheet of newsprint and a marker. Tell students to use 1 Corinthians 13 as a starting point to develop a list of good, thoughtful reasons for a couple to love one another enough to marry.

Have groups each come forward with their list, tape it to the wall and give highlights of their list. Then ask young people each to sign the list they helped develop.

OPTION 1: GOD'S LOVE FOR ME

Invite students to stand in a circle and join hands. Say: **Each person in this class is very special and God has decided to love us all. Even when we don't treat God with love, God still stays with us. As I pray the following scripture prayer from 1 John, please say the name of the person on your right when I pause. We'll say all the names in unison. Let's pray:**

This is how God showed his love for us: He sent his only son to give life through him to (Pause.)_____. **True love is not our love for God. True love is God's love for** (Pause.)_____. **God sent his son to be the way to take away our sins. Dear friends, that is how much God loves** (Pause.)_____. **So let us love each other. Amen.** (Adapted from 1 John 4:9-11.)

OPTION 2: THE LOVE PRAYER

Use the same groups from True Love. Have kids join hands in groups. Ask students each to pray silently for the person on their right while you read aloud 1 Corinthians 13. Have them include in their prayers that the person will decide to love in a way God intends.

COMMITMENT
(5 to 10 minutes)

CLOSING
(up to 5 minutes)

If You Still Have Time . . .

Saving Sex for Marriage—Play Rick Cua's song, "Young Boy Young Girl" from the album *Midnight Sun* (Reunion Records). Use it to discuss the meaning of love and the importance of committing yourself physically to one person in marriage.

Love In the Media—On newsprint, list media's messages about love and sex. Encourage kids to think of music, TV and print media. Compare that message to God's idea of love and sex.

LOVE IS MORE THAN A *Feeling*

Girls: *Love is more than a feeling.*

Guys: *Love is a decision.*

Girls: *A decision based on . . .*

Guys: *More than an attraction to a person,*

Girls: *Love is a careful process*

Guys: *Of reasoning and commitment.*

Girls: *You think it through.*

Guys: *You weigh all the facts.*

Girls: *You make a conscious choice.*

Guys: *Marriages based on feelings alone*

Girls: *Stand on dangerous ground.*

Guys: *That's because feelings can—and will—change.*

Girls: *But a love based on a decision and commitment*

Guys: *Will withstand the changing winds of feelings.*

Girls: *God shows us how to love each other;*

Guys: *God sticks by us no matter what,*

Girls: *Through all sorts of feelings.*

Guys: *That's God's unconditional love.*

Girls: *Love is more than a feeling.*

Guys: *Love is a decision.*

PERFECT LOVE—OR NOT?

Cut apart each case study and give it to "couples" and "counselors" to discuss.

Fear: "Nobody else will have me."

Their Story: Barry and Jennifer are unsure of themselves. Although they've dated for only five months, they each secretly fear this may be their one and only chance of finding a mate who'll say yes to marriage.

Scriptural Guidance:
- Psalm 139:1-5, 23-24
- 1 Corinthians 1:25
- 1 Corinthians 7:8-9
- Colossians 3:12-17
- James 1:2-5
- 1 John 4:11-19

Couple #1

Fear: Ropes may get too old to tie the knot.

Their Story: Meredith and Josh have experienced many relationships since high school. But now both of them have made "getting married" their #1 goal. They fear—at their age—if they don't get married now they'll be too old to ever marry.

Scriptural Guidance:
- Psalm 139:1-5, 23-24
- 1 Corinthians 1:25
- 1 Corinthians 13:1-13
- 1 Corinthians 7:8-9
- Colossians 3:12-17
- James 1:2-5
- 1 John 4:11-19

Couple #2

Fear: Baby on board

Their Story: Mike and Claudia have been sexually involved ever since their second date. Claudia is now two months pregnant. She was sure getting pregnant would convince Mike to marry her. They both fear the scorn of family and friends if they don't marry.

Scriptural Guidance:
- Isaiah 40:31
- Luke 14:28-30
- 1 Corinthians 13:1-13
- 2 Corinthians 4:16-18
- Colossians 3:12-17
- James 1:2-5
- 1 John 4:11-19

Couple #3

Fear: Rumors in the closet

Their Story: Craig and Vicki haven't dated much at all before meeting each other. They endured friends and family teasing them saying, "What's the matter, don't you like the opposite sex?" Both fear the label of homosexual, so they figure now's their chance to get married and put the teasing to rest.

Scriptural Guidance:
- Psalm 139:1-5, 23-24
- 1 Corinthians 1:25
- 1 Corinthians 13:1-13
- 1 Corinthians 7:8-9
- James 1:2-5
- 1 John 4:11-19

Couple #4

LESSON 4

MARRIAGE IS . . .

Not long ago, USA Today reported that "a successful marriage is more important than a job or money to today's high school student leaders." That's exciting! And the church can be the leader in helping kids find fulfillment and success if they choose to marry. One way to help kids is to give them a realistic picture of God's plan for marriage.

LESSON AIM

To help senior highers define marriage as God intended.

OBJECTIVES

Students will:
- experience the joy and frustration of being connected with someone;
- compare a good marriage to God's relationship with us.
- celebrate God's commitment to us.

BIBLE BASIS

GENESIS 2:24
EPHESIANS 5:21-33

Look up the following scriptures. Then read the background paragraphs to see how the passages relate to your senior highers.

In **Genesis 2:24**, the basis for marriage is described.

In this verse, God's institution of marriage is described as the author speaks of a man leaving his father and mother and becoming one with his wife.

It's important for teenagers to see that when couples make a wedding vow, they're promising to stand beside each other through everything—no matter what happens. The idea of being "one" goes far beyond the sexual connotations. A marriage commitment means you'll be "one" in a lot of life's joys and frustrations.

In **Ephesians 5:21-33**, Paul compares a husband and wife's relationship to Christ's relationship with the church.

Christ's love for the church is immeasurable. When Paul speaks of husbands and wives loving each other as Christ loves the church, he's emphasizing the importance of love in a marriage relationship.

Teenagers are forming friendship bonds more and more. They're ready to learn what makes good relationships tick. These verses bring up the key issues in relating as a Christian husband and wife. Respect, uphold and love each other—just like Christ loves the church.

THIS LESSON AT A GLANCE

Section	Minutes	What Students Will Do	Supplies
Opener (Option 1)	up to 5	**A Weird Wedding**—Help write a story about an unusual wedding.	Pencil
(Option 2)		**What Marriage Means to Me**—Talk about what marriage means.	
Action and Reflection	10 to 15	**The Love Connection**—Play a game and discuss situations that occur in marriage.	"The Love Connection" handout (p. 42), scissors
Bible Application	10 to 15	**God's Plan**—Complete a handout and discuss what God intended for marriage.	"A God Look at Marriage" handouts (p. 43), markers, newsprint
Commitment	10 to 15	**A Ring Ceremony**—Participate in a ceremony of commitment.	Lifesavers candy
Closing (Option 1)	5 to 10	**The Light of Marriage**—Compare the light of a candle to the joy of a Christian marriage.	Large candle, matches, small candles
(Option 2)		**Taking the Cake!**—Enjoy a surprise cake and celebrate God's plan for marriage.	Cake, serving supplies, plates, utensils

The Lesson

OPTION 1: A WEIRD WEDDING

Tell the students they're going to help write a story about an unusual wedding. Before reading the following story, ask the kids to suggest names and words you'll fill in at each blank. They won't know the context for their answers until they hear you read the story. Don't read the story aloud until you've filled in all the blanks.

Begin by asking students for the name of a girl in your class. Write in the name on the first blank in the "Weird

OPENER
(up to 5 minutes)

Wedding" box below. Then ask for a color, and so on. Keep going until all blanks are filled. Then with your most dramatic voice, read the story aloud. Or ask one of the hams in your class to do the reading.

Weird Wedding

This is the story of a beautiful young couple who decided to tie the knot on a lovely spring day. The young bride named _TANA_ (a girl in your class) giggled and practiced her pucker as she slipped into her stunning _RED_ (a color) lace wedding dress. At the same time the handsome young groom named _ERIK_ (a guy in your class) snapped on his suspenders and pinned a fragrant _DANDELION_ (flower, plant or weed) to his lapel. The wedding at _FREE METHODIST CHURCH_ (name of church in your town) was about to begin.

Everyone in town showed up for this most important of ceremonies. Everybody, that is, except _Glenn Wiley_ (name of someone in your church), who only that morning at breakfast choked on a _FLEA_ (insect or small animal) and had to remain at home and soak his _NOSE_ (a body part) in a solution of _SYRUP_ (a liquid) and _PIZZA_ (a food).

The bride's family and friends sat on one side of the church and the groom's on the other. As the organist delicately played _CAN'T TOUCH THIS_ (name of a song), the bride walked slowly down the aisle. Her beauty dazzled all. Her hair shone like a _PENNY_ (something shiny). To the lucky groom she looked like _STEVE LARGENT_ (a famous person).

The preacher named _STEVE BOWLES_ (someone in your class) nervously read the vows from _FARMERS ALMANAC_ (name of a book). The bride and groom traded adoring glances. Then came the time for the ring. The handsome groom reached into his _SOCKS_ (an article of clothing) and pulled out the ring. He gingerly placed it on the bride's lovely _FOOT_ (a body part). She shed a small tear and placed a ring upon his strong _TOE_ (a body part). And then they embraced with a _EAST_ (adjective) kiss.

The wedding was done! They were now husband and wife. They strode out of the church, and happy well-wishers threw handfuls of _PENCIL_ (small objects) upon this fine couple. They climbed into their _CHEVY_ (a make of car or truck) and sped off to their honeymoon hideaway in _WEYRHOUSER_ (a well-known-but-not-too-nice place in the area) to begin their life of wedded bliss.

Say: **Maybe our weird wedding was a bit silly. But sometimes people do like to make fun of weddings and marriage. During this lesson we'll take a close look at what God really intended marriage to be.**

OPTION 2: WHAT MARRIAGE MEANS TO ME

If your group is larger than eight, form several groups. Have each person complete the sentence, "Marriage to me means . . ."

After everyone has contributed one or more definitions of marriage, say: **Marriage means a lot of things to different people. During this lesson we'll focus on what God had in mind when he came up with the whole idea of marriage!**

THE LOVE CONNECTION

Have kids each find a partner of the opposite sex if possible. If you have an uneven number of kids, have one young person read game directions with you—or you can become a partner for the young person and play along.

Set boundaries at both ends of the room. Have all couples stand shoulder to shoulder at one end of the room, forming a line. If you have any same-sex couples, decide who'll be the guy and who'll be the girl. Have the guy in the first couple be "A" and the girl be "B." Then in the second couple, have the guy be "C" and the girl be "D." Alternate couples with either A and B, or C and D as you go down the line.

Say: **All of you who are an A—your name is Abe. Whenever you hear something about Abe, follow the directions given. All the B people, your name is Bea. Listen for Bea's instructions. Next, if you're a C, your name is Cecil. And all the D's are named Dee Dee—what else?**

As couples, you're both about to make a great commitment to each other. You're going to stay together no matter what. Let's make that promise right now.

Have partners face each other. Have kids repeat together after each line:

I,   (name)   ,
take you (partner's name)   ,
to be my awfully wedded game partner.
To have and to hold from this moment forward,
For better or worse,
In sickness and in health,
For richer or poorer,
To love, honor, cherish and generally be nice,
'Til the game is over.

Have couples hold hands. Tell them the object is to stay together as much as possible during the game and make it to the other end of the room. They'll get directions that could bring their marriage together or tear it apart.

Cut apart the instructions from "The Love Connection" handout (p. 42). Randomly pick one strip and read the instructions aloud. Continue until all strips have been read or a couple makes it across the finish line.

After the game, have partners answer these questions:
● **How did you feel during the game?**
● **How is that like what happens in real-life marriages?**
● **Why do the traditional wedding vows say things like "for better or worse, in sickness and in health"? How relevant are those vows to what goes on in marriages?**
● **What did the situations have in common that brought couples together?**
● **What did the situations have in common that broke couples apart?**
● **What did you learn about marriage that you'd like to remember for the future?**

After partners have discussed, encourage students to share

ACTION AND REFLECTION
(10 to 15 minutes)

discoveries with the whole group.

Have partners tell each other one thing they really enjoyed about being that person's partner.

BIBLE APPLICATION
(10 to 15 minutes)

GOD'S PLAN

Ask a volunteer to read aloud Genesis 2:24. Say: **God meant for marriage to be the ultimate in "oneness" for two human beings. He planned for a man and a woman to have a special kind of commitment in marriage. Throughout scripture God compares his relationship with us to a marriage. God's perfect example of love helps us see what a perfect marriage might be like.**

Form groups of three or four. Give groups the handout, "A God Look at Marriage" (p. 43) and markers. Have groups work together to read the passages and color in the word squares that best describe what the verses talk about. While students are working, draw a larger version of the handout on newsprint. Fill this in after the kids share their discoveries from their individual handouts.

The verses match up like this: Matthew 11:28-30 (helpful); Matthew 18:21-35 (forgiving); Matthew 28:20b (totally committed); Romans 5:8 (loves unconditionally); 1 Thessalonians 5:17 (in constant communication); and Hebrews 13:5b (loyal).

When groups finish, have them tell you which squares were filled in. Fill in your larger version as they answer.

Then ask:

● **What shape did the marriage verses take?** (The shape of a cross.)

● **What significance does the cross have?** (It shows the sacrifices you make when you really love someone; good marriages are ones that have Christ in the center.)

● **How is a marriage like Jesus' relationship to us?** (He loves us unconditionally; Jesus sticks by us through all the things a wedding vow promises.)

COMMITMENT
(10 to 15 minutes)

A RING CEREMONY

Have students stand in a circle and turn to face a partner. Make sure everyone has a partner; if not, pair up with a student. Say: **We've learned a lot about marriage these past few weeks. Whether you can predict now if you'll marry in the future doesn't matter. What does matter is living in the love and commitment of Jesus Christ. The greatest example of love and commitment comes through God's love in Christ. Jesus is our model and teacher for faithfulness. So we're going to celebrate that eternal love and commitment right now.**

One of the symbols of eternal love is the ring. That's why people exchange rings in wedding ceremonies. I'll be giving each of you a "ring," a Lifesaver, that you'll be

giving to your partner as part of our commitment ceremony celebrating God's commitment to us.

Ask for silence as you hand out the rings.

Say: **Face your partner and decide who'll be first to repeat after me.** (Pause.) **First, look at your partner and say
your partner's name.** (Pause.) **Now repeat after me:**

With this ring, (Pause.)

God pledges his love and faithfulness. (Pause.)

God is committed to you forever. (Pause.)

Say: **Please give your partner the ring. Now it's the
other person's turn. Look at your partner and say your
partner's name.** (Pause.) **Now repeat after me:**

With this ring, (Pause.)

God pledges his love and faithfulness. (Pause.)

God is committed to you forever. (Pause.)

Please give your partner the ring.

OPTION 1: THE LIGHT OF MARRIAGE

Form a circle around a free-standing lighted candle. Have
kids compare the light to the joy and goodness of a Christian
marriage that revolves around God's light. Give each person a
small candle (birthday candles would work). Turn out the
lights. Have kids each, one by one, light their candle and say
a prayer concerning marriage. For example, "Help strengthen
my parent's marriage," "Guide me in finding the right partner" or "Help me feel fulfilled if I stay single." When finished,
thank students for participating in the course.

OPTION 2: TAKING THE CAKE!

Bring out a surprise cake. The more it looks like a wedding
cake the better! Invite students to join hands in a circle.

Pray: **God, we're grateful you've designed what perfect
marriages can be. Help us each make good decisions and
guide us in our future—whether we plan to marry or remain single. We celebrate your love. Amen.**

Tell students to each grab a partner. Feed each other a
piece of cake! Thank each person specifically for his or her
contribution to the course.

Love, Trust, Commitment.

CLOSING
(5 to 10 minutes)

*What do you feel are
important in a
marriage?*

*What would you look
for in a marriage
partner?*

Compare commitments.

If You Still Have Time . . .

Who's Hosea?—Spend time reading and discussing the book of Hosea. Talk about God's relationship
to us in comparison to that story.

Course Reflection—Form a circle. Ask students to reflect on the past four lessons. Have them take
turns completing the following sentences:

● Something I learned in this course was . . .
● If I could tell my friends about this course, I'd say . . .
● Something I'll do differently because of this course is . . .

THE  CONNECTION

Cut each direction apart. Place the strips in a pile and draw one at a time to read aloud.

● Abe and Bea discover both of them love ballroom dancing. They sign up for a class together. Both Abe and Bea take one giant step forward.

● Abe and Bea attend a class on conflict resolution and learn how to iron out their struggles—and still love each other! Both Abe and Bea take one giant step forward.

● Abe and Bea decide to have a morning prayer time together. Both Abe and Bea take one giant step forward.

● Bea knows Abe loves homemade bread, so she bakes him a loaf! Both Abe and Bea take one giant step forward.

● Abe gets a job closer to home so he and Bea can spend more family time together. Both Abe and Bea take one giant step forward.

● Cecil and Dee Dee have always wanted children. They just discovered they're pregnant. Both Cecil and Dee Dee take one giant step forward.

● Cecil and Dee Dee decide to schedule a monthly "date" to do something fun—just the two of them! Both Cecil and Dee Dee take one giant step forward.

● Cecil apologizes for leaving his underwear on the floor. He promises not to do it again. Both Cecil and Dee Dee take one giant step forward.

● Cecil and Dee Dee have been having marital problems. But they go to a Christian counselor and work out their differences. Both Cecil and Dee Dee take one giant step forward.

● Cecil surprises Dee Dee with a dozen red roses. Both Cecil and Dee Dee take one giant step forward.

● Abe buys a motorcycle without talking to Bea about it first. Only Abe takes one giant step backward.

● Abe and Bea disagree on how often to make love. Abe takes a giant step backward and Bea takes one giant step forward.

● Bea tries to drown her problems in alcohol. Only Bea takes one giant step backward.

● Abe won't help with any of the household chores. Only Abe takes one giant step backward.

● Bea gains 50 pounds and Abe no longer finds her attractive in her bikini. Abe takes one giant step backward and Bea takes one giant step forward.

● Dee Dee refuses to get rid of her cat—which makes Cecil sneeze. Only Dee Dee takes one giant step backward.

● Cecil decides this "church stuff" is stupid and refuses to go to church with Dee Dee. Only Cecil takes one giant step backward.

● Cecil wants to spend three nights out with "the guys" every week. Dee Dee disapproves. Only Cecil takes one giant step backward.

● Dee Dee refuses to shave her legs, which Cecil finds repulsive. Dee Dee takes one giant step backward and Cecil takes one giant step forward.

● Cecil and Dee Dee never talk out their problems. They hold them all inside and then explode inappropriately. Dee Dee takes one giant step forward and Cecil takes one giant step backward.

A GOD LOOK AT MARRIAGE

Read the following verses and color in the square that contains the word that best fits the message of the verse.

- Matthew 11:28-30
- Matthew 18:21-35
- Matthew 28:20b

- Romans 5:8
- 1 Thessalonians 5:17
- Hebrews 13:5b

Good-Looking	Loves Unconditionally	Great Personality
Loyal	In Constant Communication	Helpful
Rich	Forgiving	Talented
Intelligent	Totally Committed	Popular

When you're finished, read Ephesians 5:21.
How does someone's relationship with Jesus show itself in a marriage?

BONUS IDEAS

I Do, I Do!—If possible, take the class to the musical *I Do, I DO*. It's a delightful story of one couple as they progress through their married life. Have kids discuss the musical afterward.

Song of Songs—Have kids open their Bibles to the Song of Songs. For fun, have an uninhibited guy and girl read the verses as a dialogue between the two of them. It's quite a romantic and sensual peek at the Bible. Don't forget to discuss the feelings the class has after they read it.

Divorce Discussion—Ask people who've been divorced to tell their stories. Have them complete the following statement: "If I knew then what I know now, I'd have . . ."

The Panel Approach—Bring in a panel of married people representing different stages of married life. For example:
1. Engaged;
2. Just had their first child;
3. Middle-aged with teenagers; and
4. Elderly with kids who've grown up and moved out.
Have teenagers prepare questions ahead of time to ask the panel members.

The Experts—Ask a marriage counselor or your senior pastor to come to the class and talk about the top five issues they see facing marriage today.

The Unusual Approach—Tell students about the following actual newspaper report:
Dee Dazis and Jeff Clayton vowed at their wedding to love and to obey, to have and to hold, and to rock and roll.
A Methodist minister administered Christian vows. But the man of the cloth had to share the altar in Charlotte, N.C., with Clayton's "destructo-rock" band Anti-Seen, which played a screeching rendition of the wedding march. It was billed as "the Anti-Wedding."
The 20-year-old bride and her bridesmaids wore black, as did most of the 150 or so guests. The groom had about $2^{1}/_{2}$ feet of hair. The best man was a woman. The father of the bride wore a sweater. The flower girl was a man who dumped a handful of rose petals into the lap of a family member.
The ceremony took place within the graffiti-covered walls of the 4808 Club, a former warehouse turned nightclub.
"I would have preferred a church, yes," said the groom's

mother, Ruth Clayton. "But it's his wedding, and it's what he wanted."

The groom, however, did give in to his family's wishes and wear a suit and tie.

Ask:

- **What's the purpose of a wedding?**
- **Who's a wedding for?**
- **Is there anything that should be held sacred in a wedding ceremony?**

Top Qualities in a Mate—Give students the "Top Qualities in a Mate" handout (p. 46). Have them complete the handout and then discuss it in groups of no more than five.

Table Talk—Use the "Table Talk" handout (p. 27) as the basis for a parents and teenagers' meeting. Invite parents to join their teenagers in a time of fun activities and thoughtful discussion on the subject of marriage. Include fun crowd-breakers and group-building activities to start the evening. For crowdbreakers and group-building ideas check out *Quick Crowdbreakers and Games for Youth Groups* and *Building Community in Youth Groups* (both Group Books).

Decisions About Marriage—Help senior highers learn about good decision-making in relationships. Plan a retreat that walks teenagers through decisions they're making now about sex and dating—and what consequences those decisions will have in their future.

As a guide for the weekend, get copies of the book *He Gave Her Roses* (Teenage Books). When you get six or more copies you receive a free leaders guide with creative activities, discussion questions and scripture studies.

He Gave Her Roses features a unique approach because kids choose which direction the main character takes. It's a fun and fascinating way to learn Christian decision-making. And it provides 24 different endings to the story!

Wedding Party—Have teenagers plan a party around a wedding theme. Have kids dress up as if they were either attending a wedding or getting married themselves. Serve punch and wedding cake for refreshments. Play popular songs about love and commitment, and have kids discuss the meaning of the songs.

RETREAT IDEA

PARTY PLEASER

Top Qualities IN A MATE

Read all 10 qualities. Then star five qualities you feel are most important to you for a mate to exhibit. Next rank the five starred items 1 through 5 (1=most important to you).

Place a star (*) in this column		Place ranking in this column
	Similar attitude about money	
	Good looks	
	Similar church background	
	Intelligence	
	Sense of humor	
	Athletic ability	
	Likes the same things I do	
	Easy to talk with	
	Good personality	
	Comes from a "good" family	

More from Group's Active Bible Curriculum

Yes, I want scripture-based learning that blasts away boredom.

For Senior High

Quantity

_____ 202-1 **Getting Along With Parents**
Help senior highers build quality relationships with their parents
ISBN 1-55945-202-1 $6.95

_____ 200-5 **Hazardous to Your Health**
Train senior high students to understand and avoid abusive lifestyles
ISBN 1-55945-200-5 $6.95

_____ 203-X **Is Marriage In Your Future?**
Help teenagers learn what they need to know now—so they can have a successful marriage and family life later
ISBN 1-55945-203-X $6.95

_____ 205-6 **Knowing God's Will**
Help teenagers discover God's will for their lives
ISBN 1-55945-205-6 $6.95

_____ 201-3 **School Struggles**
Train teenagers to turn school stress into school success
ISBN 1-55945-201-3 $6.95

_____ 204-8 **Your Life as a Disciple**
Help Christian teenagers develop a desire to serve God
ISBN 1-55945-204-8 $6.95

For Junior High/Middle School

Quantity

_____ 100-9 **Boosting Self-Esteem**
Help kids develop a positive self-image
ISBN 1-55945-100-9 $6.95

_____ 102-5 **Evil and the Occult**
Train junior highers to protect themselves against the trap of Satanism
ISBN 1-55945-102-5 $6.95

_____ 103-3 **Peer Pressure**
Teach students to make good decisions while keeping their friends
ISBN 1-55945-103-3 $6.95

_____ 104-1 **Prayer**
Help young people discover God through prayer
ISBN 1-55945-104-1 $6.95

_____ 101-7 **Today's Music: Good or Bad?**
Help teenagers make good decisions about music
ISBN 1-55945-101-7 $6.95

_____ 105-X **What's A Christian?**
Teach Christian teenagers the basics of their faith
ISBN 1-55945-105-X $6.95

Yes, please send me _____ of Group's Active Bible Curriculum™ studies at $6.95 each plus $3 postage and handling per order. Colorado residents add 3% sales tax.

03151

▶ ☐ Check enclosed ☐ VISA ☐ MasterCard
Credit card # _____
Good until _____

(Please print)
Name_____
Address _____
City _____ State _____ ZIP _____
Daytime phone (____) _____

Take this order form or a photocopy to your favorite Christian bookstore. Or mail to:

Group Books Active Bible Curriculum
Box 481 ● Loveland, CO 80539 ● (303) 669-3836

Blast away boredom with these upcoming scripture-based topics.

For Senior High

- Sexuality
- Making Decisions
- Materialism

- Dangers Around Us: New Age and Cults
- Being a Servant
- Injustice

- Belief-Studies in John
- Resurrection
- Faith in Tough Times

For Junior High

- Temptation: Drugs and Alcohol
- Independence
- Body-Health

- Communicating With Parents
- Relationships: Guys and Girls
- Sharing Your Faith

- Anger
- Creation
- The Bible

For more details write:

Group's Active Bible Curriculum
Box 481 ● Loveland, CO 80539 ● 800-747-6060